DATE DUE

Great African Americans

Ralph J. Bunche

peacemaker

Revised Edition

Patricia and Fredrick McKissack

Series Consultant
Dr. Russell L. Adams, Chairman
Department of Afro-American Studies, Howard University

Enslow Publishers, Inc.

40 Industrial Road	PO Box 38
Box 398	Aldershot
Berkeley Heights, NJ 07922	Hants GU12 6BP
USA	UK

http://www.enslow.com

For Nancy and Paul Polette

Revised edition of *Ralph J. Bunche: Peacemaker* © 1991

Library of Congress Cataloging-in-Publication Data

McKissack, Pat, 1944-
    Ralph J. Bunche : peacemaker / Patricia and Fredrick McKissack. — Rev. ed.
    — (Great African Americans)
    Includes index.
    Summary: Biography of the African-American statesman and diplomat who was one of the founders of the United Nations and who received the Nobel Prize for his peacemaking efforts.
    ISBN 0-7660-1701-X
    1. Bunche, Ralph J. (Ralph Johnson), 1904–1971—Juvenile literature. 2. Statesmen—United States—Biography—Juvenile literature. 3. African Americans—Biography—Juvenile literature. 4. United Nations—Biography—Juvenile literature. 5. Nobel Prizes—Biography—Juvenile literature [1. Bunche, Ralph J. (Ralph Johnson), 1904–1971. 2. Statesmen. 3. African Americans—Biography. 4. Nobel Prizes—Biography.] I. McKissack, Fredrick. II. Title.
    E748.B885 M38   2001
    973'.0496073'0092—dc21
                                00-013086

Printed in the United States of America

10 9 8 7 6 5 4

To Our Readers
We have done our best to make sure all Internet addresses in this book were active and appropriate when we went to press. However, the author and the publisher have no control over and assume no liability for the material available on those Internet sites or on other Web sites they may link to. Any comments or suggestions can be sent by e-mail to comments@enslow.com or to the address on the back cover.

Every effort has been made to locate all copyright holders of materials used in this book.
If any errors or omissions have occurred, corrections will be made in future editions of this book.

Illustration Credits: © Bettmann/CORBIS, pp. 6, 10, 13, 17; © Corel Corporation, pp. 16, 24; Department of Special Collections, Charles E. Young Research Library, UCLA, pp. 8, 11B, 15, 21; Enslow Publishers, Inc., p. 18; Library of Congress, pp. 7, 11T, 12, 20; National Archives, p. 27; Photographs and Prints Division, Schomburg Center for Research in Black Culture, The New York Public Library, Astor, Lenox and Tilden Foundations, p. 25; Stamp Design © 1982 U.S. Postal Services. Reproduced with permission. All rights reserved, p. 30; UN/DPI photo, pp. 3, 4, 22, 26.

Cover Credits: Department of Special Collections, Charles E. Young Research Library, UCLA; Library of Congress; National Archives; UN/DPI photo.

TABLE OF CONTENTS

Ralph J. Bunche
August 7, 1904–December 9, 1971

highest in his class. He was sure he would be asked to join the honor society. Ralph listened for his name. It wasn't called. He was so upset that he wanted to quit school. Nana wouldn't hear of it! "You are as good as anybody," she said.

Unfair rules kept black and white people apart. But Nana told Ralph, "You are as good as anybody."

Ralph, second row, right, had the top grades in the Jefferson High School class of 1922.

Ralph graduated from Jefferson High School with highest honors. He gave the class speech.

Nana had been right. Being poor had not stopped Ralph. Losing his parents had not stopped him. The color of his skin had not stopped him. What a wonderful world!

C H A P T E R 2

A Real Winner

Ralph's good grades helped him get into the University of California at Los Angeles (UCLA). He worked hard and studied long hours. And he was a winner in most things he tried.

Ralph played on the UCLA basketball team. It was a winning team. Ralph liked to help his team win. He was a member of other school clubs and groups. Again his grades were very good, so he finished UCLA with highest honors—another victory!

Ralph liked sports. He played basketball, baseball, and football in college at UCLA.

Then on to Harvard . . . maybe! His good grades won Ralph the money to attend Harvard University in Massachusetts. But it was not enough to pay for books, food, or rent. He would not be able to go to school.

A woman's club in Los Angeles raised $1,000 for Ralph to go to school. In the fall of 1927, Ralph entered Harvard. There he worked hard and studied long hours. Nana wrote often. Then Aunt Nelle called to say Nana had died. It was a very sad time. He would always remember his loving Nana's words, "You are as good as anybody."

In 1928, Ralph Bunche finished

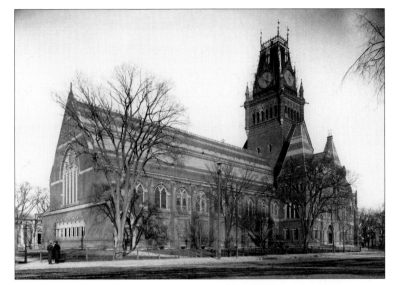

At Harvard University, left, Ralph studied government. In the photo below, he is third from the left.

his studies in government. Then he began teaching at Howard University in Washington, D.C.

That's where he met Ruth Harris, a pretty schoolteacher. Soon he won her heart, and they were married in the spring of 1930.

In 1928, Ralph was hired to teach at Howard University.

Ralph Bunche was happy. He felt like a real winner!

Ralph and
his wife,
Ruth,
had two
daughters,
Joan, right,
and Jane.

CHAPTER 3

Nations for Peace

Between 1932 and 1934, Ralph went to school in Africa. Ralph's long studies and hard work in Africa and at Harvard University earned him a Ph.D. This advanced degree is also called a doctorate. Now he could be called Dr. Ralph Bunche.

Dr. Bunche had studied a subject called political science. It is the study of governments. Dr. Bunche was the first African American to earn a Ph.D. in political science from Harvard. Nana would have been so proud.

Dr. Bunche wanted to learn more about Africa. An African friend told him to visit his people, the Kikuyu (key-KOO-yu). The Kikuyu live in Kenya, an East African country. Dr. Bunche went there.

The Kikuyu treated Dr. Bunche like a son who had been lost. He told them that his family had come from Africa a long time ago. The Kikuyu gave Dr. Bunche a Kikuyu name: Karioki (Ka-ree-o-kee), which means, "He who has returned from the dead." It was like a big party to say, "You have come home."

Dr. Bunche, right, met with many African leaders. He studied all over Africa.

15

Then, in 1939, World War II began. The countries of the world were at war. In 1941, Dr. Bunche was asked to work for the government. He was hired because the State Department needed to know about Africa during the war. At last, in 1945, the war ended.

Dr. Bunche helped write a list of goals for the new United Nations.

Millions of people died in the war. Millions more were sure to die if the world did not work to keep peace. Between 1944 and 1946, the United Nations (UN) was begun. Many nations came together for peace. Dr. Bunche had a part in the founding of the United Nations.

It was decided that the home of the UN would be in New York City. Dr. Bunche was asked to work at the UN. So the Bunches moved to New York.

In December 1948, Ruth and Ralph Bunche went to Europe. They took Ralph Jr., who was five years old.

During World War II, millions of Jews had been put to death. The Jewish people had no country of their own. The United Nations set aside a piece of land for the Jews. This was to become the country of Israel.

There were many people living in and around Israel who did not want Israel to become a country. Five Arab countries attacked Israel in the spring of 1948. There was war in the Holy Land.

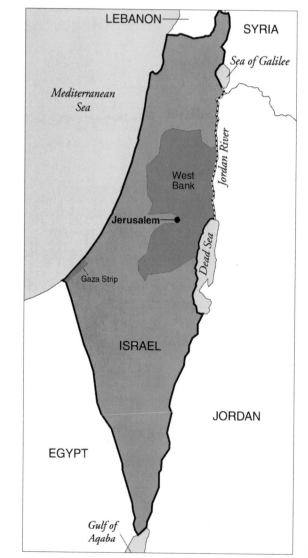

Israel and the Arab nations around it were at war.

CHAPTER 4

Peace Gets a Chance

t he Arab-Israeli War was the first real test of the United Nations. Could the UN really help stop wars? The leaders at the UN put together the best team they could. Count Folke Bernadotte from Sweden led the team. Dr. Bunche was chosen to help Count Bernadotte.

The count asked the Israelis and the Arabs to meet on a Greek island. He wanted them to talk about peace. They would not come. But the count didn't give up. Peace must get a chance. It took four weeks, but the armies stopped fighting at last. It was a beginning. Would peace last?

Then, in September 1948, Count Bernadotte was killed. Would his death stop the peace talks? It was a dark day for peace. The world was sad.

Dr. Bunche was asked to keep working for peace. War between Israel and the Arabs started again. But Dr. Bunche didn't give up. Peace must get a chance.

Dr. Bunche worked hard for peace between the Arabs and the Israelis.

There were months and months of talking. Finally the Israelis and the Arabs ended the war. A peace treaty was signed.

Peace at last!

Dr. Bunche gave each Israeli and Arab at

The UN sent soldiers to the Middle East to keep peace. Dr. Bunche visited them in 1949.

21

Dr. Bunche also worked for peace in Africa. This meeting was held on an airplane.

the meeting a peace gift—a beautiful piece of pottery. "What if we had not made peace?" one of the Israelis asked.

"I would have hit you over the head with them," Dr. Bunche answered, smiling. Then everyone laughed.

Peace would get a chance at last.

CHAPTER 5

He Was the First

B eing at home with his wife, Ruth, and his family meant more to Dr. Bunche than being well known. But he was a hero. People loved him. They wanted to meet him and to hear him speak. Pictures of Dr. Bunche and his family were in newspapers and on the covers of magazines.

Los Angeles had a Ralph Bunche Day and a big parade. His name was added to the city honor society. It would have meant so much more to him if his name had been added in 1922, when he was the top student at his high school. But he smiled and said, "Thank you."

The NAACP gave Dr. Bunche its top honor, the Spingarn Medal. The next year, he won the Nobel Peace Prize, below.

Winning a Nobel Peace Prize is one of the highest honors given in the world. In 1950, Ralph Bunche won the Nobel Peace Prize for helping end the war in the Holy Land. He was the first African American to win this high honor.

He was also given the Gold Key Award by the National Education Association. Dr. Bunche was asked to name his favorite teacher. Who else but Miss Emma Belle Sweet!

Dear Daddy
I am happy
you got the
Nobel peace
Prize
Love
Ralph

Joan and Ralph Jr. were so proud when their father won the Nobel Peace Prize.

25

Was Miss Sweet still alive? Yes. She was eighty-two years old. But she was able to come to receive the Gold Key given to her. Dr. Bunche got to see his favorite teacher again after forty-seven years.

Dr. Ralph Johnson Bunche worked for the UN and peace for twenty-five years. He was a man of firsts . . . the first member of his family to finish college . . . the first African American to earn a

Dr. Bunche spoke with Coretta Scott King and Martin Luther King, Jr., after Dr. King won the Nobel Prize in 1964.

Dr. Bunche was part of the civil rights March on Washington, D.C., in 1963.

Ph.D. in political science from Harvard University . . . and the first black man in the world to win the Nobel Peace Prize. He did it against all odds.

In 1971, Dr. Bunche left the UN because his health was poor. He died six months later, on December 9, 1971. The world was sad. A news reporter wrote: ". . . when all the world praises a man, there seems little left to say."

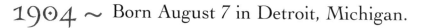

1904 ~ Born August 7 in Detroit, Michigan.

1927 ~ Graduates from the University of California at Los Angeles.

1930⊙ ~ Marries Ruth Ethel Harris.

1934 ~ Earns a Ph.D. from Harvard University.

1941 ~ Works for the government.

1945 ~ Helps write the United Nations Charter, a list of goals for the UN.

1946 ~ Attends the first session of the UN in London.

1949 ~ Helps work out a peace treaty between the Arabs and Israel. Is awarded the Spingarn Medal by the National Association for the Advancement of Colored People (NAACP).

1950⊙ ~ Wins the Nobel Peace Prize.

1955 ~ Becomes undersecretary of the United Nations.

1963 ~ Receives the Presidential Medal of Freedom.

1971 ~ Retires from the United Nations. Dies on December 9.

1927

1945

1930

WORDS TO KNOW

Arab—A member of one of the Arabic-speaking peoples who live in the Middle East and North Africa.

award—An honor given to a person for doing something special.

colored—An outdated name that was used for African Americans.

degree—A school gives a degree (a title) to students who have completed all their studies.

Gold Key Award—An honor given to a person who has done an outstanding job in the area of education.

graduate—To complete studies at a school.

Holy Land—Countries in the Middle East where the Jewish, Christian, and Islamic religions began.

honor society—a group of people who have earned very high grades in school.

NAACP (National Association for the Advancement of Colored People)—An organization started to help all Americans gain equal rights and protection under the law.

WORDS to KNOW

National Education Association—An organization of people who work in education, with teachers, principals, and others.

Nobel Peace Prize—A special honor given to a person who has worked for world peace. It is named after Alfred Nobel, a man who left money in his will to start the prize.

peace treaty—An agreement that stops war or keeps war from starting.

political science—The study of governments and how they work.

pottery—Things made of clay, such as some pots, bowls, plates, and cups.

United Nations—An organization of many countries who work together for peace.

Ralph Bunche

USA 20c

This 1982 postage stamp honors Ralph Bunche.

LEARN MORE ABOUT RALPH J. BUNCHE

Books

Armbruster, Ann. *The United Nations*. Danbury, Conn.:
   Franklin Watts, 1995.

McNair, Joseph D. *Ralph Bunche*. Chanhassen, Minn.:
   Child's World, 2001.

Schraff, Anne. *Ralph Bunche: Winner of the Nobel Peace Prize*.
   Berkeley Heights, N.J.: Enslow Publishers, Inc., 1999.

Internet Addresses

Ralph Bunche: An American Odyssey
Biography, photos, timeline
   <http://www.pbs.org/ralphbunche/>

Encyclopedia Britannica
"Ralph Bunche," articles, photos, videoclip
   <http://www.britannica.com/eb/article?eu=18332>

Stamp on Black History: Ralph Bunche
   <http://library.thinkquest.org/10320/Bunche.htm>

index